Published by Barbour Books, an imprint of Barbour Publishing, 1810 Barbour Drive, Uhrichsville, Oh 44683, www.barbourbooks.com

Our mission is to inspire the world with the life-changing message of the Bible.

Member of the
Evangelical Christian
Publishers Association

Printed in China.

06319   0219   HA

READ IT!

PRAY It!

Write It!

DRaW IT!

DO IT!

A Faith-Building Interactive Journal for Kids

BY JEAN FISCHER

BARBOUR BOOKS
An Imprint of Barbour Publishing, Inc.

CONTENTS

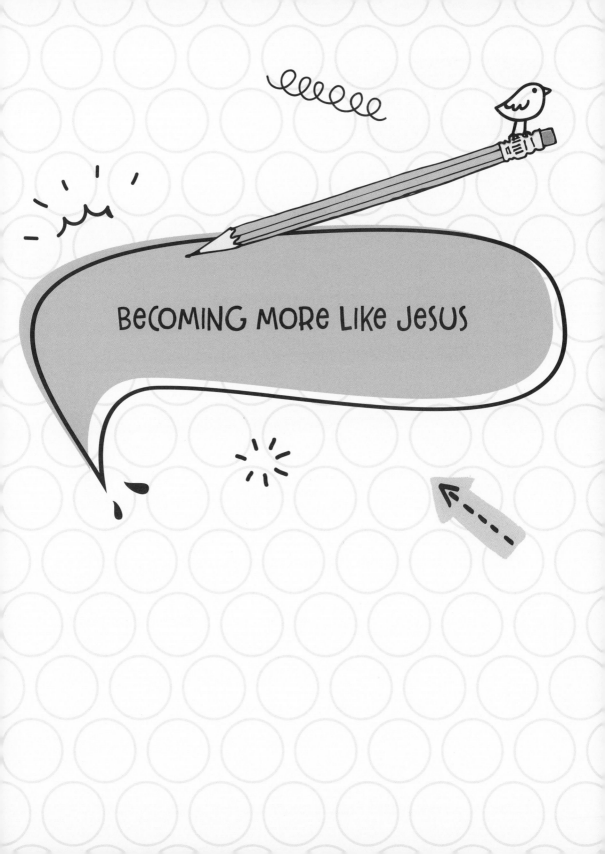

Think as Christ Jesus thought. Jesus has always been as God is. But He did not hold to His rights as God. He put aside everything that belonged to Him and made Himself the same as a servant who is owned by someone. He became human by being born as a man. After He became a man, He gave up His important place and obeyed by dying on a cross.

PHILIPPIANS 2:5–8

Who is Jesus? He is God's Son. For a while, Jesus lived here on earth with a special purpose—to make a way for people to have forever life with Him in heaven. While Jesus lived here, He had a human body like everyone else. Although He was God's Son, Jesus never acted proud or stuck-up. He was the perfect example of how humans should behave with each other: loving, forgiving, caring, and kind. He always obeyed God's rules and did what was right. Jesus was even willing to die if it meant everyone could someday live in heaven.

DEAR JESUS, I want to become more like You. Please teach me how to forgive others when they hurt me. Show me how to be caring and kind, and help me to love others even when they are hard to love. I want to do what is right. . . .

List some things you can do every day to become more like Jesus.

Draw a picture of Jesus
doing something kind.

DRaW IT!

DO IT!

Practice being more like Jesus today. Forgive someone who hurt your feelings. Do something kind and caring for a family member or friend. Say, "I love you" to someone you care about.

What did you learn from Philippians 2:5-8?

....

....

....

....

....

....

....

....

....

....

....

....

....

HOW TO GET TO HEAVEN

"For God so loved the world that He gave His only Son. Whoever puts his trust in God's Son will not be lost but will have life that lasts forever."
JOHN 3:16

Nobody's perfect. We all do things that aren't right with God. *Sin* is a word for the wrong things people do. Sin isn't allowed in heaven, so God sent His Son, Jesus, to earth on a special mission—to make a way for everyone to get to heaven.

When Jesus agreed to give up His own life by dying on a cross, He also agreed to take the punishment for everyone's sins so someday they could enter heaven sin-free! God said that whoever believes Jesus did that is promised the gift of life with Him in heaven—forever.

JESUS, YOU gave Your life so I can live in heaven someday. You died for all the sins everyone would ever do. Thank You! When I do something that displeases God, I know He forgives me, because You already took the punishment for my sin. . . .

Write about why you think Jesus was willing to give up His own life so everyone can go to heaven.

....

....

....

....

....

....

....

....

....

....

....

....

....

....

....

What do you think heaven looks like?
Draw it.

DRaW IT!

DO IT!

Memorize John 3:16: "For God so loved the world that He gave His only Son. Whoever puts his trust in God's Son will not be lost but will have life that lasts forever." Share this Bible verse with your friends. Tell them about what Jesus did.

What did you learn from John 3:16?

....

....

....

....

....

....

....

....

....

....

....

....

....

....

WHAT IS FAITH?

Because Noah had faith, he built a large boat for his family. God told him what was going to happen. His faith made him hear God speak and he obeyed. His family was saved from death because he built the boat. . . . Noah became right with God because of his faith in God.
HEBREWS 11:7

Imagine someone telling you, "A giant flood is coming to cover all of Earth. I want you to build a huge boat to hold your family and two of every kind of animal."

That's what God told Noah to do. It seemed impossible, but because Noah trusted God, he did it!

Faith means putting all our trust in God, even when we don't understand what He's doing. The Bible tells us how God wants us to live. He wants us to believe that He knows what is best for each of us and that He will *always* help us with everything.

DEAR GOD, it isn't easy trusting in things I can't see. So will You help me trust You more? You know everything! You know exactly how things will work out *before* they happen. That's why I can have faith in You to work everything out for my good. . . .

PRAY It!

Write It!

Make a list of the animals you think were on Noah's ark. See if you can list one kind of animal for each letter of the alphabet. (Hint: You might need to do some research!)

Draw a creative design using the word FAITH.

DRaW IT!

DO IT!

God shows He is faithful by *always* doing what He promises. Today, make a promise to someone. Then do what you promise. When you follow through on your promises, others will learn to have faith in you.

What did you learn from Hebrews 11:7?

....

....

....

....

....

....

....

....

....

....

....

....

....

Then Peter came to Jesus and said, "Lord, how many times may my brother sin against me and I forgive him, up to seven times?" Jesus said to him, "I tell you, not seven times but seventy times seven!"

MATTHEW 18:21–22

What do the numbers 4, 9, and 0 have to do with forgiveness? A multiplication problem is hidden in Matthew 18:21–22. Find and solve it.

Seventy times seven equals 490. Jesus told His followers to forgive those who hurt them not once. . .not twice. . .not seven times, but 490 times! He didn't mean *exactly* 490, but He did mean we should keep on forgiving—even when we don't feel like it.

God forgives us for our sins, and He wants us to do the same toward others.

FATHER GOD, when someone hurts my feelings, I might not want to forgive right away. I need Your help learning to forgive as many times as I have to. I don't think people want to be mean. It just happens sometimes. I know forgiveness is important because. . .

PRAY It!

Write It!

Think of the last person you needed to forgive. Then finish this thought.

I forgive you because. . .

....

....

....

....

....

....

....

....

....

....

....

....

....

....

....

....

....

....

....

Draw a big heart—in your favorite color—around these words: I FORGIVE YOU.

DRaW IT!

DO IT!

Take turns with a friend making up silly things that might need forgiveness.

For example:

You: *"I'm sorry that I accidentally bumped your nose with a banana."*

Your friend: *"I forgive you."*

See how long you can play without either of you laughing.

What did you learn from Matthew 18:21-22?

Love does not give up. Love is kind. Love is not jealous. Love does not put itself up as being important. Love has no pride. Love does not do the wrong thing. Love never thinks of itself. Love does not get angry. Love does not remember the suffering that comes from being hurt by someone. Love is not happy with sin. Love is happy with the truth. Love takes everything that comes without giving up. Love believes all things. Love hopes for all things. Love keeps on in all things. Love never comes to an end.

1 CORINTHIANS 13:4–8

Love is much more than hugs, kisses, and cuddles. Love is patience and kindness to the max! It is putting others first and forgiving and celebrating each other's special moments. Love is doing what is right so God will always look down on our actions with pride. It is always hoping for the best.

Love means believing in forever. When we truly love others, we love them *all the time*, even when they say and do things that make them seem unlovable. That's how God loves us—and that's how God wants us to love each other.

WOW, GOD! I didn't know that love is connected to so many things! I guess love isn't always easy. I want to love others like You love me—with a patient kind of love. Will You teach me to do that, please?. . .

Write a note to someone telling that person why you love him or her. Leave the note in a special place where the person will find it. Practice what you want to say in the space below.

Draw a picture of what love
means to you.

DRaW
IT!

DO IT!

Do something special for someone. . .something unexpected. It doesn't have to be anything big. You could go to bed on time or clean your room without being asked. Can you think of other things you can do to show your love? Remember to tell your family members that you love them. Tell them every day!

What did you learn from 1 Corinthians 13:4–8?

....

....

....

....

....

....

....

....

....

....

....

....

....

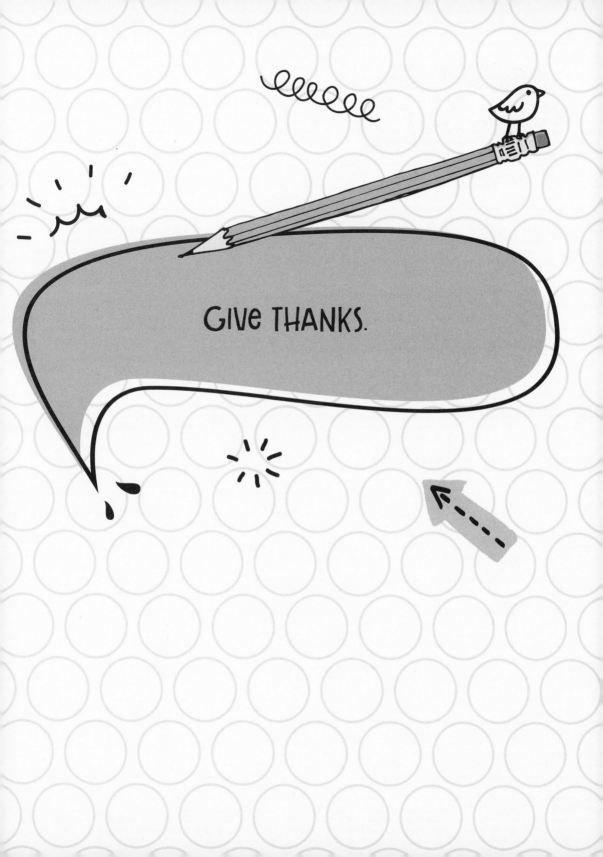

Let us give thanks all the time to God through Jesus Christ. Our gift to Him is to give thanks. Our lips should always give thanks to His name. Remember to do good and help each other. Gifts like this please God.

HEBREWS 13:15–16

Think about this: What if you made a special gift for someone? Much time and love went into making that gift. But when you gave your special present to that special someone, the person ignored it. No "thank you." No hug. Not even a smile. How would you feel?

Each day is filled with gifts from God—gifts like life, health, food, shelter, and love. And too often, we forget to thank Him.

Saying "thank you" and showing others we care is important. Get into the habit of saying "thank you" not only to God but to everyone!

DEAR GOD, when I pray, I ask You for things I want, and I also ask You to bless the people I love. But I don't spend enough time thanking You for everything You do for me. I hope You know that I'm grateful. Forgive me for the times I haven't said, "Thanks."...

PRAY It!

Write It!

Make a list of people you need to thank. Maybe they gave you a gift and you're late sending a thank-you note, or maybe someone did something nice for you and you forgot to thank him or her. Find a special way to say "thank you" to everyone on your list.

Create and decorate a thank-you card for God in the space below.

DRaW IT!

41

DO IT!

Listen for the words "thank you" today. Keep track of how many times you hear them. Did you notice times when someone deserved a thank-you, but it didn't happen?

What did you learn from Hebrews 13:15–16?

When I look up and think about Your heavens, the work of Your fingers, the moon and the stars, which You have set in their place, what is man, that. . .You care for him? . . . You made him to rule over the works of Your hands. You put all things under his feet: All sheep and cattle, all the wild animals, the birds of the air, and the fish of the sea, and all that pass through the sea. O Lord, our Lord, how great is Your name in all the earth!

PSALM 8:3–4, 6–9

Everyone has a boss, someone who is in charge. You're a kid, so your parents are the boss of you. When you get older and have a job, you will follow instructions given to you by a boss at work.

There is one Boss greater than all others. The Boss of all bosses. The Boss of everything! Can you guess who it is?

It's God! He made the earth, sky, people, animals— everything! He is in control of it all. God trusts us to help care for His creation, and He makes the rules. Nothing—no one— is greater than He!

GOD, I'M glad You are the boss, because You are so smart. You know everything about—*everything!* You know the names of all the stars in the sky. You know all the people on earth. You know everything about me too!. . .

Write It!

God is the greatest, but you're pretty great yourself. Why? Because God made you! Write a few sentences that tell what's so great about YOU.

....

....

....

....

....

....

....

....

....

....

....

....

....

....

....

....

What do you think is the greatest thing God created? Draw it here.

DRaW IT!

DO IT!

There are hundreds, thousands, *millions* of reasons why God is great. Get a beanbag or other soft object and play catch with a friend. Before you throw the object, say one reason why you think God is great. Pick up the speed. Faster. *Faster!* How long can you keep up the pace before one of you runs out of ideas?

What did you learn from Psalm 8:3-4, 6-9?

"When you pray, do not be as those who pretend to be someone they are not. They love to stand and pray in the places of worship or in the streets so people can see them. For sure, I tell you, they have all the reward they are going to get. When you pray, go into a room by yourself. After you have shut the door, pray to your Father Who is in secret. Then your Father Who sees in secret will reward you."

MATTHEW 6:5–6

Isn't it amazing that God wants to communicate with us? Prayer is how we talk with Him. When we pray, God always hears us. He especially loves times when we go someplace quiet and tell Him what's going on in our lives. When we talk with God, we should pray using our own words just like we're speaking to a very best friend. God is never too busy to listen. It's okay to talk with Him anywhere, even all day long. We don't have to pray out loud. God even hears when we say prayers silently in our heads.

DEAR GOD, thank You for loving me and wanting to hear from me. I'm grateful that You are always ready to listen when I pray. Let's spend some quiet time to-gether. I have a lot to tell You about what's going on in my life. . . .

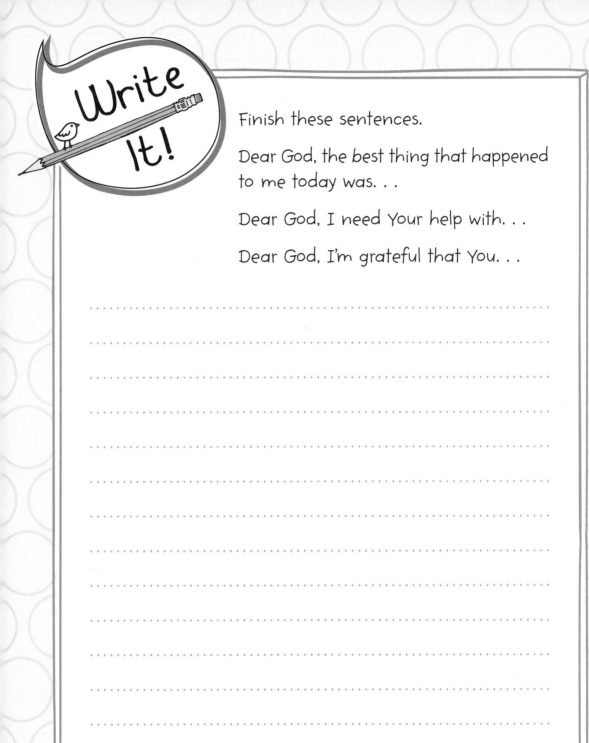

Write It!

Finish these sentences.

Dear God, the best thing that happened to me today was. . .

Dear God, I need Your help with. . .

Dear God, I'm grateful that You. . .

God wants us to pray for our family and friends. Draw two people you would like to pray for this week.

DRaW IT!

DO IT!

Find someplace in your house where you can spend quiet time with God. Think of it as your secret meeting place with Him. It doesn't have to be hidden from anyone. The secret is that only you and God know which place you've chosen.

What did you learn from Matthew 6:5-6?

....

....

....

....

....

....

....

....

....

....

....

....

....

The Lord Who bought you and saves you, the Holy One of Israel, says, "I am the Lord your God, Who teaches you to do well, Who leads you in the way you should go. If only you had listened to My Laws! Then your peace would have been like a river and your right-standing with God would have been like the waves of the sea."

ISAIAH 48:17–18

Decisions can be hard. Sometimes we must choose between things that are equally good or not-so-good. There are times when we feel confused and don't know which way to go.

Whenever we face tough choices, the first thing to do is ask God for help. He always knows exactly how we should choose. The Bible helps too. As we study it, we learn what God says is right and wrong, and that often makes choosing the right way easier. The Bible tells us to trust God, and He will show us which way to go (Proverbs 3:5–6).

FATHER GOD, You are so wonderful and wise. You always know the best thing to do and the right way to go. I need Your help making a decision. I trust You to show me what to do and lead me in the right direction. . . .

Write It!

Write about a hard choice you had to make.

....

....

....

....

....

....

....

....

....

....

....

....

....

....

....

....

....

....

....

Draw two things that you *really* love to eat. If you could have only one, which would you choose? Put an X by it.

DRaW IT!

DO IT!

Hide an object. Then give a friend some choices about how to find it. You can say things like: "Choose between going left or right." "Look up or down." "Keep going or stop."

Do you see how easy it is to mess up when you don't know which way to go?

What did you learn from Isaiah 48:17–18?

Children, as Christians, obey your parents. This is the right thing to do. Respect your father and mother. This is the first Law given that had a promise. The promise is this: If you respect your father and mother, you will live a long time and your life will be full of many good things.

EPHESIANS 6:1–3

All through the Bible, we find God making good rules for people to follow. He must think obedience is important, because when God created the first humans, He gave them rules!

The Bible says we should obey the rules made by God and also our parents. Following God's rules, along with those set by parents and other trusted adults, helps us to become strong, kind, and well-mannered grown-ups.

Sometimes we might think a rule is silly or not for us. Still, we should do our best to obey. Why? Because obedience pleases God.

GOD, PLEASE forgive me when I don't want to follow my parents' rules. Sometimes I've thought I'm too old for a rule. I've even thought a few of their rules are silly. But Your Word says I should obey and respect my parents, and that's what I want to do. . . .

Write one rule that you find hard to obey. Then write some thoughts about why it's good to follow that rule.

....
....
....
....
....
....
....
....
....
....
....
....
....
....
....
....
....

What do you think is the most important rule? Draw a picture of yourself obeying it.

DRaW IT!

DO IT!

Have a family meeting to set up some house rules. Make a list of the rules and hang it where all family members can see it. (Are any of God's rules on your list?)

What did you learn from Ephesians 6:1–3?

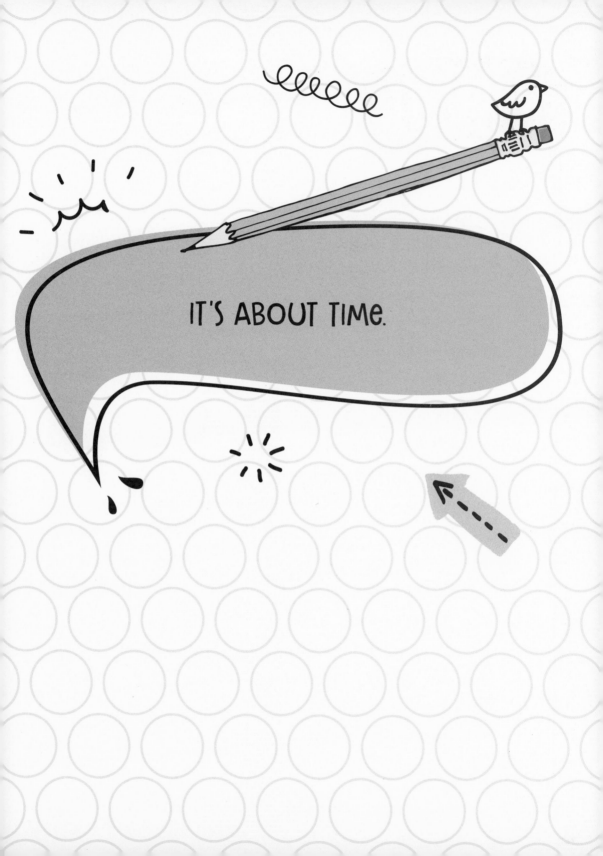

Do not throw away your trust, for your reward will be great. You must be willing to wait without giving up. After you have done what God wants you to do, God will give you what He promised you.

HEBREWS 10:35–36

When it was time for God to give the Israelites a special place to live—the Promised Land—God chose Moses to lead them. Moses might have thought the journey would take a few months or even a year. But instead, it took forty years! Along the way, Moses learned patience. He said to God, "A thousand years in Your eyes are like yesterday when it passes by, or like the hours of the night (Psalm 90:4)."

God's timing is different from ours. But He promises if we wait patiently and trust Him, He will reward us.

DEAR GOD, I hadn't thought that Your timing is different from mine. Does it really seem to You that a thousand years is like a day? I need to remember that whenever I want You to hurry up and answer my prayers. Will You help me to be more patient?...

Write It!

What are some things you can do when you feel impatient? Write your ideas here.

....

....

....

....

....

....

....

....

....

....

....

....

....

....

Are you waiting for something special?
Draw it.

DRaW IT!

Teach a younger sibling or friend to do something that's difficult for him or her. Be patient while you teach. Can you think of some gentle ways to teach patience to others?

What did you learn from Hebrews 10:35–36?

....

....

....

....

....

....

....

....

....

....

....

....

....

....

....

....

....

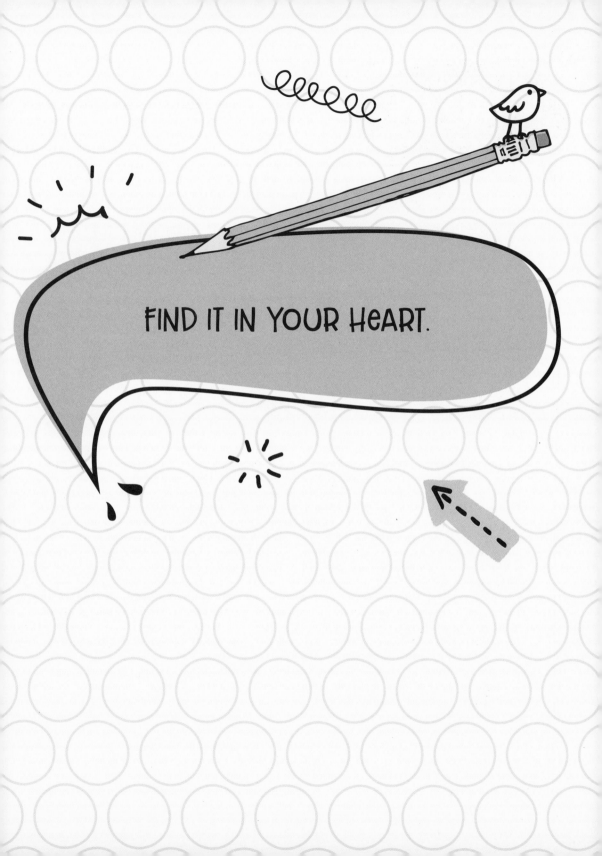

If someone has the gift of speaking words of comfort and help, he should speak. If someone has the gift of sharing what he has, he should give from a willing heart. If someone has the gift of leading other people, he should lead them. If someone has the gift of showing kindness to others, he should be happy as he does it.

ROMANS 12:8

Did you know kindness comes from the heart? God fills up our hearts with all sorts of words and ideas to use when showing kindness toward others. It's our job to search inside our hearts to find out what God put there and then to share those good things.

God wants us always to be willing to help. If we open our eyes and ears to what's going on around us, we'll discover many different ways to show kindness. It doesn't have to be something big. Sometimes a smile or a few gentle words is all someone needs.

HEAVENLY FATHER, thank You for always being kind to me, and thank You for all the good stuff You have put in my heart to help me show kindness to others. Help me to look inside my heart for ways, big and small, to share kindness. . . .

PRAY It!

Write It!

Do you know someone who could use some kindness? List some little ways you might brighten his or her day.

Draw yourself doing something kind.

DRaW IT!

DO IT!

Choose someone (a family member, teacher, or friend) to be extra-kind to today. Do little things to help and make that person feel special. Don't tell him or her why you are being so kind. Kindness done in secret is kindness straight from the heart.

What did you learn from Romans 12:8?

Then Peter said, "I can see, for sure, that God does not respect one person more than another. He is pleased with any man in any nation who honors Him and does what is right."
ACTS 10:34–35

Have you wondered if God loves some people more than others? The answer is no. God creates each person as one-of-a-kind, and He loves all people equally with His complete, powerful, and ever-lasting love. Jesus' follower, Peter, knew that. He said, "*For sure*, God does not respect (value) one person than another."

We all are God's children, and He loves each of us the same. It doesn't matter how we look, where we come from, or what we accomplish. One is not more lovable than another—and that is how God wants us to see each other.

DEAR GOD, whenever I meet someone new, remind me not to judge him or her as being better or worse than me—or anyone else! I want to value everyone equally, and I want You to be pleased with me for honoring both You and others. . . .

Write It!

Finish the sentences.

Everyone is equal because God. . .

God is pleased with everyone when they. . .

....

....

....

....

....

....

....

....

....

....

....

....

....

Draw a picture of you and a friend.
Add a heart to your drawing
and the words GOD LOVES US!

DRaW IT!

DO IT!

Do you know someone who comes from a different part of the world? See what you can find out about the country where he or she lived. And if you see kids making fun of someone's differences, step up and remind them that God loves us all the same.

What did you learn from Acts 10:34-35?

"For I know the plans I have for you," says the Lord, "plans for well-being and not for trouble, to give you a future and a hope. Then you will call upon Me and come and pray to Me, and I will listen to you. You will look for Me and find Me, when you look for Me with all your heart."

JEREMIAH 29:11–13

"Why, God? Why didn't that work out the way I wanted it to?"

Everyone sometimes asks God *why*. That's because His understanding is so much greater than ours. His plans for us are bigger than any we can imagine.

If we look back on a plan gone wrong, we often find that God moved us in a new direction for a good reason. When our plans change, we can trust that God is in control, watching over us. We can put all our hope in Him, because He loves us, and He will always lead us toward something good.

FATHER GOD, my brain is filled up with *why* questions. I wonder about so many things. Sometimes the future is scary because I don't know how it will work out. But You know, God! I feel better re-membering that You are in control and Your plans for me are good. . . .

Write It!

Write down some things you have planned for your future. Then pray about them and ask God to lead you in the right direction.

Draw yourself in the future as a grown-up. What will you look like? What will you be doing?

DRaW IT!

DO IT!

Hope is one of the most important words in Jeremiah 29:11. Hope means wanting something to come true. Do you know someone who needs something today—something they are hoping for? Can you do something to help make their hope come true?

What did you learn from Jeremiah 29:11–13?

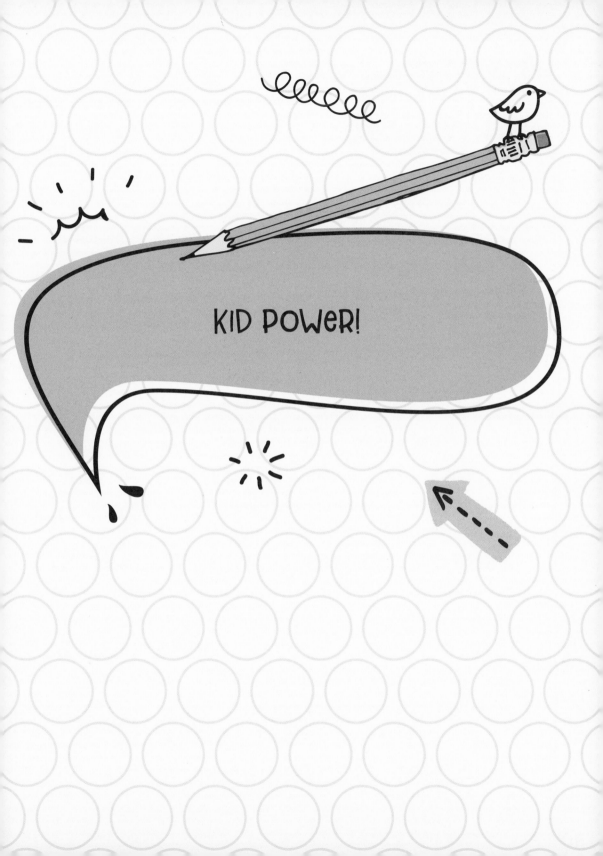

Let no one show little respect for you because you are young. Show other Christians how to live by your life. They should be able to follow you in the way you talk and in what you do. Show them how to live in faith and in love and in holy living. . . . Watch yourself how you act and what you teach. Stay true to what is right.
1 Timothy 4:12, 16

You might be a kid, but you can have a powerful—and good—effect on others. God gives you the power to show kids, and grown-ups too, how to live as Christians.

When you study the Bible, you learn how God wants you to behave toward, talk to, and love others. You can share what you learn with your family and friends by being a good example. You have *kid power*, and it's the most important kind of power—leading others to God! Don't let anyone stop you from being the best Christian you can be.

DEAR GOD, wow, I didn't know I had such power to lead—power that comes from You! I promise to learn all I can about how a Christian should behave so I can set a good example. I want my friends and family to know and follow You too. . . .

PRAY It!

Write It!

Finish this thought.

Today, I will set a good example by. . .

You have kid power that comes from God! Draw yourself as God's superhero here on earth.

DRaW IT!

Start a club with some of your friends. Make it your mission to lead others to God by setting a good example. You can do amazing things when God gives you His power.

What did you learn from 1 Timothy 4:12, 16?

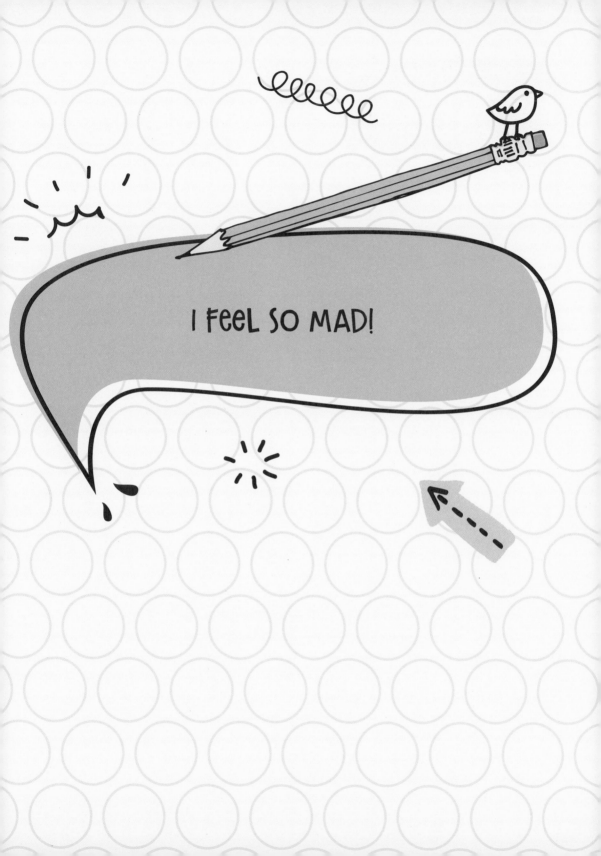

My Christian brothers, you know everyone should listen much and speak little. He should be slow to become angry. A man's anger does not allow him to be right with God.

JAMES 1:19–20

If you were a dog and got angry, you might bite someone. But before you could chomp down on a person's leg, your human would try to stop you. That's sort of how it is with us and God. When we get mad, God wants us to remember our Christian training and react in the best way—by calming down and allowing Him to handle the situation.

When we learn to manage our angry feelings and replace them with forgiveness, then we please God. He is not pleased if we react to get even or hurt someone in return.

FORGIVE ME, God, for times when I've said and done things out of anger. I'm sorry for hurting others, even if I thought they deserved it. The next time I feel angry, I'm going to come right to You and ask You to handle the situation for me. . . .

PRAY It!

Write It!

List some things you can do to calm yourself down when you feel angry.

First draw an angry face. Then draw a forgiving face. Draw an X by the face that pleases God.

D R a W IT!

DO IT!

Role-play with a sibling or friend how you might change an angry situation. Pretend that you are mad at each other. Then act out ways that you might become friendly again.

What did you learn from James 1:19–20?

....

....

....

....

....

....

....

....

....

....

....

....

....

....

....

....

....

....

....

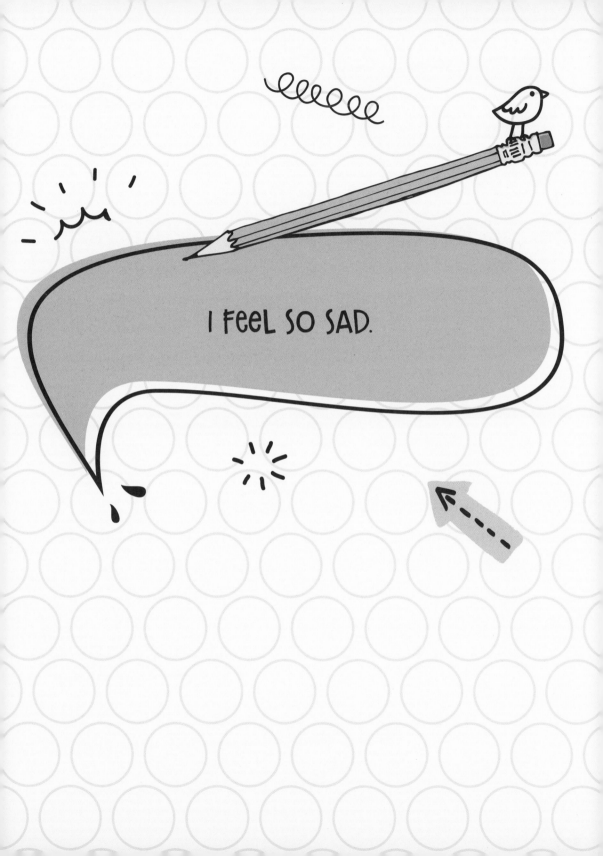

Those who are right with the Lord cry, and He hears them. And He takes them from all their troubles. The Lord is near to those who have a broken heart. And He saves those who are broken in spirit. A man who does what is right and good may have many troubles. But the Lord takes him out of them all.
PSALM 34:17–19

One of the worst feelings is sadness. It fills up our hearts and pushes out all the good stuff. God doesn't want His kids' hearts broken, so He is always ready to help. The Bible says God sees our tears, and He puts them in His bottle (Psalm 56:8). He knows our troubles, and He saves us from them all. Our job is to remember that, and to also have faith in God to help us when we feel sad. God loves His children. You might not feel it, but He wraps His arms around you whenever He sees you cry.

DEAR GOD, I hate feeling sad. It fills me up and takes any good feelings away. I know You love me, so will You please help me to feel better? Put my tears inside Your bottle. Then open my eyes to everything good and make me happy again. . . .

Write It!

Finish these sentences.

When I feel sad, I know that God. . .

I will feel better if I. . .

Draw yourself doing something fun
that makes you feel happy.

DRaW
IT!

DO IT!

Getting up and doing something active can help chase sadness away. Put on some music and dance or go outside and play. If you feel really sad, don't keep it to yourself. Tell your parent or another trusted adult, and ask them to help you.

What did you learn from Psalm 34:17–19?

READ IT!

"Do not fear, for I am with you. Do not be afraid, for I am your God. I will give you strength, and for sure I will help you. Yes, I will hold you up with My right hand that is right and good. See, all those who are angry with you will be put to shame and troubled. Those who fight against you will be as nothing and will be lost. You will look for those who argue with you, but will not find them. Those who war against you will be as nothing, as nothing at all."
Isaiah 41:10–12

The Bible tells about David, a boy who stood up to a giant soldier named Goliath. The grown-up soldiers were afraid of Goliath, but David had courage. It didn't matter that he was young. David had confidence in himself because he was right with God. And with God's help, David defeated Goliath (1 Samuel 17:1–50).

God gives us courage and strength whenever we face our own bullies or anything else that makes us afraid. Like David, we can trust in God's help. God is *always* with us.

GOD, I want to learn to stand up to trouble with the kind of courage David had. I promise to trust You to help me. Please teach me not to *be afraid* and to have confidence in myself when I know I'm doing what's right. . . .

PRAY It!

Write about a time when you felt afraid and God gave you courage.

....

....

....

....

....

....

....

....

....

....

....

....

....

....

....

....

....

....

....

....

Draw David standing strong in front of the big soldier, Goliath.

DRaW IT!

DO IT!

Is there something you'd like to do, but you're afraid because you don't feel good enough or tough enough? Give it a try! Ask a parent to help you, and then trust God to give you courage and strength.

What did you learn from Isaiah 41:10–12?

*So stop lying to each other. Tell the truth to your neighbor.
We all belong to the same body. . . . Watch your talk! No bad
words should be coming from your mouth. Say what is good.
Your words should help others grow as Christians.*

EPHESIANS 4:25, 29

No one is perfect. All humans slip up sometimes and bad words come from their mouths. A bad word isn't always a swear word. Bad words can be any words that communicate a lie or unkind things about others.

The talk that comes from our mouths should be truthful and kind. It should build others up and make them feel good about themselves. Whenever we slip up and say something to hurt someone, or something we know displeases God, we should be quick to recognize our bad words and follow them up with, "I'm sorry."

I NEED to watch my words, God. Sometimes I don't think before I speak. I mess up and say things I don't mean. I'm sorry. Forgive me. Help me choose words that please You. Remind me to always say what's true and to say kind things about others. . . .

Write It!

What is the nicest thing anyone has ever said to you? Write it here.

Use these words to make a
creative design:
GOOD   KIND   TRUE   WORDS

DRaW
IT!

Play this Compliments Game with a friend. Take turns saying kind things—compliments—about each other. See if you each can come up with ten things. Can you play the game a second time without repeating what you said in game one?

What did you learn from Ephesians 4:25, 29?

WHAT IS SELF-CONTROL?

But the fruit that comes from having the Holy Spirit in our lives is: love, joy, peace, not giving up, being kind, being good, having faith, being gentle, and being the boss over our own desires.
GALATIANS 5:22–23

Self-control means you are the boss of your behavior when you can't have what you want.

God's Spirit—the Holy Spirit—helps with that. When we really, *really* want something we can't have, we can rely on God to help make us strong. When we learn self-control, then we can walk away from those things we want but can't have.

God's Holy Spirit helps us not only with self-control but other good things too like: love, joy, peace, not giving up, being kind, being good, having faith, and being gentle.

DEAR GOD, sometimes I don't behave well when I can't have what I want. I need to *be a better boss over my be-havior*. Will You help me learn how to act when I really want something but I can't have it? Will You teach me self-control?. . .

Write It!

Finish the sentences.

When I don't get what I want, I feel. . .

Self-control means. . .

Draw a picture of something you have that you *really* love. Then draw yourself in the picture walking away from it.

DRaW IT!

DO IT!

Aside from controlling your behavior, self-control can also mean doing what is right—even when it's not what you want to do. A great way to learn that kind of self-control is obeying without complaining when your parent asks you to do a chore. Try it. See if you can go through one whole day doing whatever your parent asks—without grumbling. Remember to rely on God to give you strength.

What did you learn from Galatians 5:22-23?

....

....

....

....

....

....

....

....

....

....

....

DOING FOR OTHERS

"Do good to those who hate you. Respect and give thanks for those who try to bring bad to you. Pray for those who make it very hard for you. . . . Give to any person who asks you for something. If a person takes something from you, do not ask for it back. Do for other people what you would like to have them do for you."

LUKE 6:27–28, 30–31

Jesus had good advice for treating others the right way. He said, "Do for other people what you would like to have them do for you."

We want people to be good to us, respect us, and give thanks for us. We want others to pray for us and be generous toward us—even when we aren't behaving our best.

When we think about how we want to be treated, it helps us learn right from wrong. When we treat others as we want to be treated, then we are doing what's right.

FATHER GOD, thank You for Jesus! He gives such good advice, and He's gentle and kind while teaching me. I don't always remember to treat others the way I want to be treated, so I'm going to try even harder. I'm going to memorize what Jesus said, and do it!. . .

Write It!

Make a list of how you want others to treat you. (You can write things like, *I want them to be kind.*) See how many ideas you can add to your list.

Jesus said, "Do for other people what you would like to have them do for you." Draw a picture of you doing something nice for a friend.

DRaW IT!

DO IT!

Memorize Luke 6:31: "*Do for other people what you would like to have them do for you.*" Then use the list you wrote (on page 130), and practice treating others the way you want them to treat you.

What did you learn from Luke 6:27–28, 30–31?

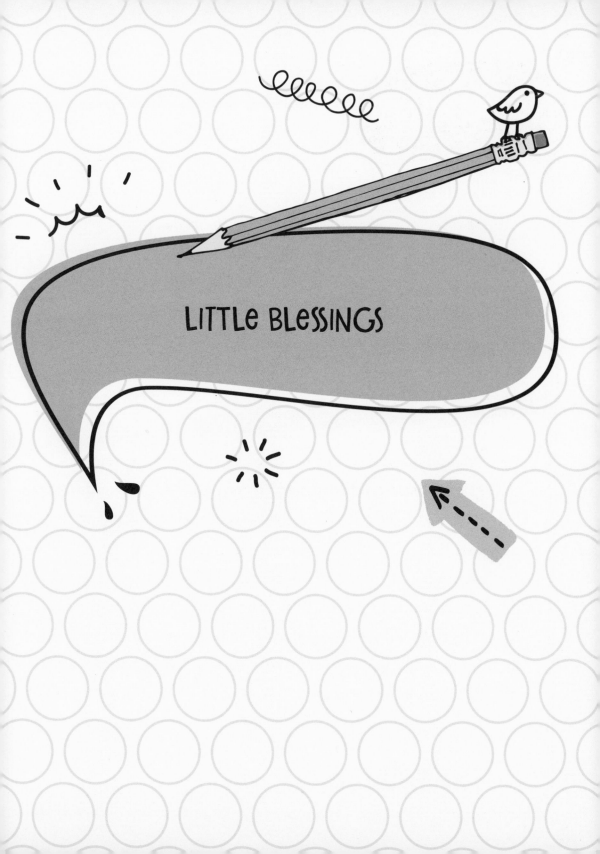

At this time Jesus was full of the joy of the Holy Spirit. He said, "I thank You, Father, Lord of heaven and earth. You have kept these things hidden from the wise and from those who have much learning. You have shown them to little children. Yes, Father, it was what you wanted done."
LUKE 10:21

People can become so busy with work and other worries that they don't notice all the amazing things God does. Things like God's love and His caring for us can get buried among all the other stuff.

God wants us to notice all the good He does for us every day, and especially the little hidden things, like keeping our hearts beating, our lungs breathing, our eyes seeing. Every day, God hides many wonderful little blessings for us to discover. It's our job to find them—and we will, if we ask God to help us.

GOD, WHAT blessings have you hidden for me to find? Open my eyes and ears to all the little things. Show me what You've tucked away, inside and out. You never hide things so I can't find them. Usually they are in plain sight, so please show me where to look. . . .

....

....

....

....

....

....

....

....

....

....

....

....

....

....

Write It!

Write a few sentences about something new you saw or learned.

....

....

....

....

....

....

....

....

....

....

....

....

....

....

....

God has placed wonderful little blessings in gardens among the flowers. Draw a garden picture showing those "hidden" blessings.

DRaW IT!

Ask your parent to go with you on a nature walk in the woods, on the beach, or some- place else. Look for little hidden things God put there: wildflowers, bugs, animals, pretty rocks. . . How many different little blessings can you and your parent find?

What did you learn from Luke 10:21?

. . . .

. . . .

. . . .

. . . .

. . . .

. . . .

. . . .

. . . .

. . . .

. . . .

. . . .

. . . .

GOD'S TALENT SHOW

God has given each of you a gift. Use it to help each other. This will show God's loving-favor. If a man preaches, let him do it with God speaking through him. If a man helps others, let him do it with the strength God gives. So in all things God may be honored through Jesus Christ. Shining-greatness and power belong to Him forever. Let it be so.
1 PETER 4:10–11

Everyone has something he or she does well. It's true! God made each of us with special talents we can share with others.

A talent doesn't necessarily mean a person can play a musical instrument, sing, dance, or create art. There are many other kinds of talents—like wisdom, teaching, and being a good and caring helper.

We can ask God to show us the talents we were born with and to help us make them grow. Whatever we are good at, we should always use our talents to bring goodness to others.

DEAR GOD, thanks for giving me special talents. One of the best things is that, as I get older, I'll find even more things I'm good at! I'm sure You've hidden some talents inside me that I haven't discovered yet. I can't wait to find out what they are!. . .

Write It!

Write about one thing you're really good at. Then explain how you might share your talent with others.

Draw yourself trying something new—something you hope to be good at.

DRaW IT!

DO IT!

The Bible says we should use our special talents to help others. Have a family meeting to discuss how your family can combine its talents to do something nice for someone. For example, one of you might be good at baking cookies, another at putting them in a pretty package, someone else at making a cheerful card, and so on. . . .

What did you learn from 1 Peter 4:10–11?

....

....

....

....

....

....

....

....

....

....

....

....

When I kept quiet about my sin, my bones wasted away from crying all day long. For day and night Your hand was heavy upon me. My strength was dried up as in the hot summer. I told my sin to You. I did not hide my wrong-doing. I said, "I will tell my sins to the Lord." And You forgave the guilt of my sin.
PSALM 32:3–5

Sometimes people do things they know are wrong, and they get away with it. But then, they feel guilty. That nasty little secret sin is like a seed planted inside them, and before long it grows into embarrassment and shame.

Getting away with something bad is never good! Sin disappoints God, and He is even more disappointed when sin is kept secret.

But there's good news! God forgives our sins all the time! He doesn't keep track of them either. We only need to pray, tell Him what we did, and ask for His forgiveness.

DEAR FATHER in heaven, I'm ashamed to tell You that I did something I knew was wrong, and I got away with it. I'm truly sorry for disappointing You. Please forgive me. I'm going to do everything I can to make up for what I did. . . .

PRAY It!

Write It!

Think of a time you did something you knew was wrong. Write God a little note asking Him to forgive You. You can trust that He will!

....

....

....

....

....

....

....

....

....

....

....

....

....

....

Draw a face showing how someone feels when he or she has done something wrong. Draw another face showing how someone feels when he or she is forgiven.

DRaW IT!

DO IT!

Everyone sins. No one is perfect. When you say your prayers every day, get in the habit of telling your sins to God. You don't have to be afraid. He loves you! God understands that kids mess up sometimes, and He is always quick to forgive.

What did you learn from Psalm 32:3-5?

....

....

....

....

....

....

....

....

....

....

....

....

You are as right and good as mountains are big. You are as fair when You judge as a sea is deep. O Lord, You keep safe both man and animal. Of what great worth is Your loving-kindness, O God! The children of men come and are safe in the shadow of Your wings.

PSALM 36:6–7

Whatever happens, we can feel safe with God. Even in the worst situations, God promises to be with us—and He always keeps His promises. We might not feel God's presence, but He's there. The Bible says He watches over both people and animals.

If you've ever seen a mother hen protect her chicks, you know she keeps them safe under her wings. That's how the Bible describes God. He can make you feel safe, no matter what! Whenever you feel unsafe, God will take care of you.

DEAR GOD, thank You for always watching over me and helping me feel safe. I don't know how You can *be* everywhere at the same time, but You can! I never have to worry that You are busy with someone else. You promise to *be* with me all the time. . . .

Write It!

Finish the sentences.

I feel safest when. . .

I know God watches over me because. . .

Draw something you were afraid of when you were younger, but you are not afraid of now.

DRaW IT!

DO IT!

Memorize these Bible verses. Say them to yourself whenever you feel afraid.

When I am afraid, I will trust in [God].
PSALM 56:3

[God says:]

Do not fear, for I am with you. Do not be afraid, for I am your God. I will give you strength, and for sure I will help you.
ISAIAH 41:10

What did you learn from Psalm 36:6-7?

....

....

....

....

....

....

....

....

....

....

....

It is the same for all. The same thing will happen to both the man who is good and the man who is sinful. The same thing will happen to the clean and the unclean, and to the man who gives a gift on the altar and to the man who does not. As the good man is, so is the sinner. As the man who swears is, so is the one who is afraid to swear.

ECCLESIASTES 9:2

Why does bad stuff happen to good people? That's a question everyone asks.

When God created the first humans, Adam and Eve, He gave them the right to make their own decisions—to choose between good and evil. Making the wrong choice allowed sin to enter the world.

God still gives people the right to choose, and wrong choices sometimes lead to bad things happening to those who are good. Life isn't always fair. But God promises to help His children through the bad stuff. Remember: God loves you all the time and nothing can separate you from His love.

GOD, I want to make right choices. Give me wisdom to know right from wrong. Help me to do my best to obey Your rules and the rules my parents give me. Remind me that the wrong choices I make can affect not only me but others too. . . .

Write It!

List three good choices and explain what makes them good.

Next, list three choices you know are wrong and explain what makes them wrong.

Draw yourself choosing
to do what is right.

DRaW
IT!

DO IT!

Play this game with a friend.

Take turns giving each other two choices. You can mix serious ideas (*Would you rather run into the street with your eyes closed or look both ways before you cross?*) with silly ideas (*Would you rather eat broccoli or a bee?*). Decide which choice is best and discuss why.

What did you learn from Ecclesiastes 9:2?

A man who has friends must be a friend,
but there is a friend who stays nearer than a brother.
PROVERBS 18:24

God didn't want us to be lonely, so He put others in our lives: parents and grandparents to help us grow up; teachers to help us learn about the world; pastors to teach us about Him; and friends to have fun with. And God gave us the best friend ever: Jesus!

Friends are important. They share the best times of our lives with us. The Bible says to have a friend, we first need to *be* a good friend. When we are kind, helpful, and caring toward others, then they will want to join us in friendship.

DEAR GOD, thank You for my friends! We have a lot of fun together. I hope that I am as good a friend to them as they are to me. Keep showing me how to be the best kind of friend, and thank You for my best friend, Jesus. . . .

Write It!

Write a few sentences telling why you think you are a good friend.

Draw a picture of your best friend.

DRaW
IT!

See if you can make a new friend this week. At school, ask someone to sit with you at lunch or to play with you at recess. What other ways can you think of to find new friends?

What did you learn from Proverbs 18:24?

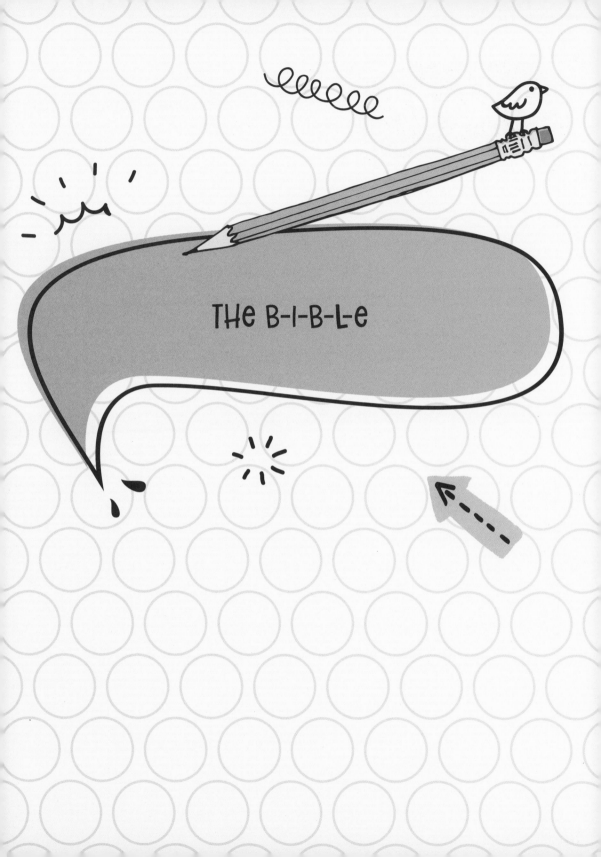

READ IT!

Understand this first: No part of the Holy Writings was ever made up by any man. No part of the Holy Writings came long ago because of what man wanted to write. But holy men who belonged to God spoke what the Holy Spirit told them.
2 PETER 1:20–21

The Bible is also called "God's Word." That's because God's Spirit created it. God gave certain men the words to write, and those words have been passed down in the Bible.

The Bible helps us know right from wrong. It leads us to make good decisions. It also gives us all the information we need to be right with God (2 Timothy 3:16–17). As we read and study the Bible, we learn what God expects from us, and we also discover that Jesus is the only way to heaven.

How often do you read the Bible?

I THINK it's awesome, God, that You gave us Your book, the Bible. I like learning from its stories. The more I read my Bible, the more I find out about You! There's always something new to discover—something that shows me how powerful, kind, and loving You are. . . .

Write It!

Finish the thought.

The Bible is important because. . .

....

....

....

....

....

....

....

....

....

....

....

....

....

....

....

....

Draw a scene from your
favorite Bible story.

DRaW
IT!

DO IT!

Get in the habit of reading the Bible every day. Ask your parent to help you find and memorize some of its most important verses. If you hold some of God's Word in your memory, then you can recall it whenever you need His help.

What did you learn from 2 Peter 1:20–21?

....
....
....
....
....
....
....
....
....
....
....
....
....
....
....
....

READ IT!

[Jesus] said to them, "You are to go to all the world and preach the Good News to every person. He who puts his trust in Me and is baptized will be saved from the punishment of sin. But he who does not put his trust in Me is guilty and will be punished forever."

MARK 16:15–16

Jesus told His followers to share the Good News with everyone on earth. The Good News is that God sent His Son, Jesus, into the world to save us all from being punished for the wrong things we do. We need to be made perfect to enter heaven, and believing that Jesus took the punishment for our sins makes us perfectly ready to live with God in heaven someday.

If we trust that Jesus died for our sins, then God promises us forever life in heaven. So—share the Good News with family and friends. Tell them about Jesus.

DEAR GOD, please give me the words to tell my family and friends about how Jesus is the only way to heaven. Help me to teach them that if they believe Jesus died for their sins, then they will live forever in heaven after they die. . . .

Write It!

Fill in the blanks.

God sent His Son _____ to earth.

_____ died on the cross and took the punishment everyone deserved for their sins.

If we believe that _____ took the punishment for our sins, then we will live forever in _____ after we die.

....

....

....

....

....

....

....

....

....

What do you imagine Jesus looks like?
Draw Him.

DRaW IT!

DO IT!

Spread the Good News! Don't be afraid to tell others that you know Jesus. He wants to be friends not only with you but with everyone on earth!

What did you learn from Mark 16:15–16?

....

....

....

....

....

....

....

....

....

....

....

....

....

....

....

....

....

....

For by His loving-favor you have been saved from the punishment of sin through faith. It is not by anything you have done. It is a gift of God. It is not given to you because you worked for it. If you could work for it, you would be proud.

EPHESIANS 2:8–9

God could have made us work hard to get to heaven. But instead He sent us a special gift—a worry-free way to heaven—Jesus!

God is so very good to us, and we don't deserve His goodness. We disappoint Him every day by making wrong choices. But God loves us so much that when we sin He shows us grace. *Grace* is a word that means God continues to love and forgive us even when we don't deserve it!

We can be like God and show grace toward others by always being forgiving and kind.

YOU ARE so good to me, God! I don't have to do anything for You to love me. You love me all the time! You bless me every day with so many wonderful things. Thank You for Your grace, and please help me to show grace toward others. . . .

Write It!

List some ways you can show grace toward someone who is behaving badly.

Write the word GRACE in a colorful design.

DRaW IT!

DO IT!

Thanking God for His grace and showing grace toward others are important, but so is showing grace toward yourself. Learn to take responsibility for the wrong decisions you make, and forgive yourself for those decisions. Why? Because God forgives you! He wants you to love yourself because He loves you.

What did you learn from Ephesians 2:8–9?

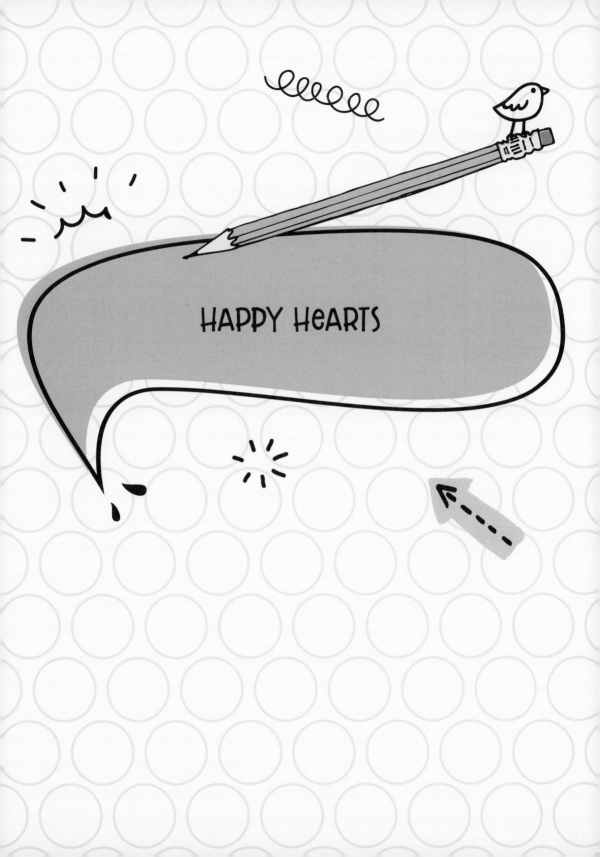

Be filled with joy while you are young. And let your heart be happy while you are a young man. Follow the ways of your heart and the desires of your eyes. But know that God will judge you for all these things. So put away trouble from your heart. . . . Because the years when you were a child and the best years of your life are going by fast.
ECCLESIASTES 11:9–10

When Jesus lived on earth, He told His disciples to always allow children to come to Him. Jesus loved kids. He liked having them around. He even used a young boy to help with a miracle. (Read about it in John 6:1–14.)

God wants kids to be happy and have fun. But while they are having fun, God expects them to do their best to make right choices and obey. When kids share, behave, and play nice with each other, it pleases God. That kind of play leads to happy hearts. Have fun and enjoy being a kid!

THANKS, GOD, for all the fun You've put in the world. I'm grateful for toys, games, places to visit, and, most of all, I'm thankful for friends to play with. I hope how I choose to have fun pleases You, because I want You to have a happy heart too. . . .

Write It!

Write about the most fun you ever had with your friends.

Draw you and your friends playing together.

DRaW IT!

191

DO IT!

Ask a parent to help you plan something special you can do with your friends. Think of new ways you can have fun together. Then, when you say your prayers, remember to thank God for your friends, fun, and a happy heart.

What did you learn from Ecclesiastes 11:9–10?

....

....

....

....

....

....

....

....

....

....

....

....

....